# ABANDONED
# FLORIDA
## SUNSHINE SENTINELS

### THOMAS KENNING

AMERICA
THROUGH TIME®
ADDING COLOR TO AMERICAN HISTORY

*For Rory. May you always find something
down the beach that's worth exploring*

America Through Time is an imprint of Fonthill Media LLC
www.through-time.com
office@through-time.com

Published by Arcadia Publishing by arrangement with Fonthill Media LLC
For all general information, please contact Arcadia Publishing:
Telephone: 843-853-2070
Fax: 843-853-0044
E-mail: sales@arcadiapublishing.com
For customer service and orders:
Toll-Free 1-888-313-2665

www.arcadiapublishing.com

First published 2020

ISBN 978-1-63499-269-5

Typeset in Trade Gothic
Printed and bound in England

# CONTENTS

*If the hail rattles, let the flowers be crushed—the stately oak of the forest will lift its head to the sky and the storm, towering and unscathed.*

Osceola, vowing to defend Seminole Florida against foreign conquest, 1834

# INTRODUCTION

# SUNSHINE SENTINELS

F lorida has a longer coastline than any other state in the contiguous United States—an estimated 1,350 miles of low-slung sand, mangroves, and coveted beachfront real estate. Since the arrival of the Spanish more than four centuries ago, that vast shoreline has proven to be the peninsula's greatest asset—and its greatest vulnerability.

Right from the start, easy access to the sea made the frontier outpost of *San Agustín* a crucial safe harbor for ships plying the often perilous maritime routes linking Spain's transatlantic empire. But this same accessibility also made the faint village a tempting target for rival European powers, eager to establish their own North American toehold. Thus, the Spanish tinkered for decades to ensure that Florida's oldest-standing coastal fortress, the formidable Castillo de San Marcos, remained state-of-the-art, even as the sands of time shifted around it.

Centuries later, the United States grappled with the same fundamental dilemma as the Spanish. Through continual experimentation, they chased the ever-changing answer to the question—is it possible to effectively defend Florida's long coast from a sometimes ill-defined rogues' gallery of hostile hosts, each with suspected intentions far more sinister than a simple holiday in the sun?

That's where *Abandoned Florida: Sunshine Sentinels* picks up the thread, presenting the colorful histories of seven of Florida's abandoned coastal defenses—ranging from the coquina confines of the *castillo* to the towering casemates of far-flung Fort Jefferson in the Dry Tortugas; from Fort Barrancas, which looms in the heights over shattered Fort Pickens in Pensacola to the cracked concrete batteries of Fort Dade in Tampa Bay; from the carefree garden spot of West Martello Tower in Key West to the paranoia-making, nuclear-powered HM-69 Nike Missile Base deep in the Everglades.

A few of Florida's historic coastal fortifications—Fort Clinch and Fort Zachary Taylor, for example—didn't make it into this volume. This omission isn't intended as a slight. They, too, have stories worth telling, but in the interest of producing a photographically-rich history that's still streamlined enough to fit comfortably in your hands, their turn in the spotlight will have to wait. There's easily enough material out there for a second volume on Florida's abandoned coastal defenses, provided there's interest enough to warrant one.

Finally, it's worth noting that this book is already something of a historical document itself. The photos reproduced within comprise a warts-and-all portrait of these crumbling behemoths as they exist today, roughly a quarter of the way through the twenty-first century. But it's an open question as to how much longer they might persist, even in this diminished form. Every one of these coastal defenses—sitting almost by definition mere feet above the lapping waves—will be irrevocably impacted by rising sea levels in the not-too-distant future.

I can't say it emphatically enough: if you haven't already, you should get out there and see these stately sunshine sentinels for yourself, while you still can. Even better, do your part to beat back the rising tide of climate change. It would be a shame if, after all the effort expended by previous generations of Floridians in defense of this magnificent land, we were the ones to let it slip into the sea without so much as a fight.

Thomas Kenning
Sunny Florida, July 2020

# 1

# CASTILLO DE SAN MARCOS,
## ST. AUGUSTINE

Initial construction of the Castillo de San Marcos commenced in 1672. The fort was designed by Ignacio Daza to replace a succession of nine wooden forts which had defended San Agustín since its founding in 1565.

In the game of "America's First, Best, Most," Castillo de San Marcos in St. Augustine is Florida's ace. The revolution may have unfolded at Lexington and Yorktown, but St. Augustine hosts the oldest masonry fort in the oldest continuously inhabited European settlement in what is today the United States. If you squint right, in a certain light, the American story starts here, in rough-hewn *coquina*.

At least, that's the story they're selling to the six million or so tourists who visit St. Augustine each year.

The Spanish began construction of the present fort in 1672, after a previous wooden structure was burned to the ground by English pirates. The soft stone was quarried and laid by Native American laborers from nearby missions—their holy tithe, in the eyes of the Spanish, tantamount to slave labor in the minds of the natives themselves, no doubt.

Between then and now, the *castillo* has seen far more action than most forts in Florida, successfully repelling several sieges by the English, but ultimately changing between Spanish, British, American, and Confederate hands half a dozen times.

The forbidding Castillo de San Marcos faces outward toward the sea, the first coastal bastion of the European colonial project in America. Ironically, under the Americans, rechristened Fort Marion, its most important function was as a prison—a heavy hand against the fiercest Native American resistance from within the continent. The Americans retrofitted storerooms in its thick, sedimentary walls into a full-service dungeon.

The *castillo's* walls are composed of 400,000 hand-cut blocks of *coquina*, a porous, sedimentary stone that compresses upon impact, which gave the fort a remarkable resilience to cannon fire. This *coquina* was once covered by a neat layer of red and white plaster.

At the base, the *castillo's* walls range in thickness between fourteen and nineteen feet. Renovations undertaken by the Spanish between 1738 and 1756 brought the walls to their current height of thirty-five feet.

The plaza de armas—or parade ground—hosted two centuries of Spanish garrisons in performance of musket drills and other training exercises. It also provided refuge to the population of St. Augustine, on one occasion sheltering 1,500 soldiers and civilians for nearly two months during the English siege of 1702.

The *castillo* is comprised of four diamond-shaped bastions. Clockwise from the northeast they are San Carlos, San Agustin, San Pedro, and San Pablo. Taken together with the fort's curtain walls, these bastions allowed a defending force to cast a web of interlocking crossfire.

In 1837, during the Second Seminole War, the great Chief Osceola was captured by the United States Army under a false flag of peace. He would become Fort Marion's most famous inmate. Beginning in 1875, dozens of leaders from the Apache, Kiowa, Cheyenne, and other western tribes would follow in his unhappy footsteps. Some processed their captivity by creating evocative, colorful sketches on ledger paper cast off by the fort's administrators. Overcrowding meant that many of these prisoners camped in tents on the parade ground.

The American story had come full circle. After centuries of westward conquest, in an act of desperation, the United States resorted to deporting the most independent-minded natives back east to Florida, to a frontier long since settled—imprisoning them in walls built by their distant cousins under the Spanish lash so many years earlier.

This isn't the only story at Castillo de San Marcos, of course. It's a problematic one, though, perhaps better suited for the middle chapter of some book. It doesn't leave anyone feeling particularly good. It's a harder sell than the one you already know—the one told in a much louder voice throughout St. Augustine.

Turns out that conquistadors and pirates go better with ice cream cones—any more specific brand of American violence leaves a bad aftertaste.

The ravelin is a triangular structure guarding the *castillo's* sally port—its only entrance. Though the ravelin was never completed—it was intended to be taller with a crenellated parapet—it sufficed to shield the relatively weak wooden doors of the sally port from direct enemy fire.

The *castillo* is surrounded by a man-made slope called a glacis. The glacis put any attacking force at a disadvantage, forcing it to fight uphill under a hail of fire originating from the gundeck or from the covered way, the additional defensive position that caps the glacis.

The moat that sits inside the covered way once surrounded the *castillo* on four sides. It was kept dry as a pen for livestock, but could be flooded rapidly with sea water if necessary.

Between 1842 and 1844, the Americans filled the fourth side of the moat in order to construct a water battery. This fortification provided an additional layer of defense from enemy guns as well as a firing position for larger caliber American guns developed during the nineteenth century.

The gundeck of the *castillo* was armed with dozens of cannons, howitzers, and mortars firing shots ranging in weight between sixteen and twenty-four pounds. The largest guns could hurl these projectiles to a maximum distance of three-and-a-half miles, creating an umbrella of defense over the mouth of Matanzas Bay.

Each bastion is filled solid with sand and other debris, which serves as an additional bulwark against enemy assault. This infill also provides support for up to ten large weapons on the gun deck above, each weighing in the neighborhood of 3,000 pounds.

The tallest tower—on San Carlos bastion—provides an unimpeded view of the entrance to Matanzas Bay. It once housed an upper platform for the soldier on watch as well as a bell to alert the surrounding town in the event of impending attack, likely from the English or the French.

Britain acquired Spanish Florida in the Seven Years War. During the Revolutionary War, the colony remained loyal to the crown, providing an important base for British operations in the southern colonies. As a nominal ally of the fledgling United States, Spain recaptured Florida before the end of the war—only to lose it once and for all several decades later, this time to the U.S.

◄ St. Augustine was an important cog in the machine of Spanish Empire. It offered convoys of galleons, laden with the ill-gotten treasures of the Caribbean, Mexico, and Peru, their last chance at safe harbor before riding the westerlies home to the European continent.

It is by night that Castillo de San Marcos best reveals its true character—both out-of-time and of-its-place, an accretion of characteristics from across continents and centuries, its *coquina* block awash in electric light, cracked and weatherworn, saturated with the blood of conquest and conflict.

Under Spanish rule, the *castillo* became a beacon of hope for Africans enslaved by the English. If these runaways could successfully make their way south to Florida, they would be welcomed in either St. Augustine proper or, later, at nearby Fort Mose, the first free black settlement in the future United States.

The Spanish weren't any more enlightened on race than the English—they simply suspected that the Carolinas might be destabilized by a steady southern exodus of slave labor. Fort Mose was founded by decree of the royal governor in 1738, at which time St. Augustine's free black population was forcibly relocated there. In its twenty years of existence, Fort Mose attracted thousands of ex-slaves.

There is little to see of Fort Mose's wood and earthen defensive works today—it was perpetually the target of English attack, and the Spanish were happy to let this segregated settlement bear that burden. When the English took control of Florida in 1763, many free blacks decamped to Cuba alongside other Spanish civilians.

# 2

# FORT JEFFERSON,
## DRY TORTUGAS

Visitors to the Dry Tortugas arrive by ferry, seaplane, or private vessel. Two of these sightseers stand atop the northwest bastion of Fort Jefferson (1846), fifty feet above the Gulf of Mexico on the open upper level of the fort known as the barbette tier.

Seventy miles beyond Key West lies a sandy chain of islands devoid of any freshwater. These desert islands make an ideal sanctuary for hundreds of nesting sea turtles and ocean birds. Collectively, they are the aptly-named Dry Tortugas. The shallows that dominate the floor of the Gulf between here and Key West are a natural minefield, slashed where small boats have run aground and scarred with the shipwrecks of those possessed of a deeper draft and less luck.

In centuries past, most ships in transit between the northern Gulf and the Atlantic would naturally hew to the navigable passage of deep water that brings them within a cannonball's shot of these lonely keys.

Thus, the quixotic Fort Jefferson, a floating fortress, Florida's first theme park—a military fantasia in brick and mortar, comprised of sixteen million blocks forming a two-tiered hexagonal structure complete with firing positions for 420 large guns, arranged so that 125 of them could zero on the same target simultaneously. Its eight-acre parade had room for two massive powder magazines, a three-story thousand-man barracks, officer quarters, and a hospital. There's also a hotshot furnace for heating cannonballs until they glowed red—the better to ignite the last generation of wooden warships, still in use when this fort was conceived.

When you see it from the air, before the window of your seaplane is misted over with a salty spray, when you can take the whole thing in at once, Fort Jefferson is an unrivaled colossus. Pure military might astride tiny Garden Key, an awesome American island in command of a wide-open sea—a projection of power that you can't help but believe.

There's the theme for your park.

From the window of a DHC-3 Otter seaplane, the fort seems to inhabit the exact middle of nowhere. In actuality, it commands a 75-mile-wide strait linking the Gulf and the Atlantic Ocean. Scores of shipwrecks dot the reefs and the vast shallows on either side of the strait

There is exactly nothing understated about Fort Jefferson, a structure that seems to have little regard for the laws of nature.

Built over the course of three decades as a part of the Third System of coastal fortifications, which itself was an ambitious but awkward adolescent phase of the United States' military ascendency, Fort Jefferson is more stagger than swagger. Its intricate cistern system never worked properly and actually managed to turn its collected rainwater salty. As at other forts in Florida, yellow fever was a serious issue from the moment that work crews of enslaved laborers arrived on Garden Key in 1846.

Even as you stand in the overgrown grass amidst cracked foundations on the parade, it's hard to believe the scale of their work—Fort Jefferson's two shortest curtain walls measure 325 feet in length, while the remaining four stretch to 477 feet. Most guns are long gone, but the 303 open-vaulted casemates remain, facing toward the sea through tattered embrasures.

This 15-inch Rodman smoothbore weighs twenty-five tons. Six such guns were installed at Fort Jefferson, one on top of each bastion. Operated by a crew of seven men, they could fire a 440-pound projectile a distance of three miles. Positions for 420 guns—most smaller than this—were planned for the fort's three levels.

The large parade magazine—the most complete of five planned—dominates the north corner of the eight-acre parade ground. Its arched roof was designed to deflect enemy cannonballs, but advances in rifled artillery—capable of penetrating its brick veneer—made it a giant Achilles heel. It never saw service.

The open casemates of the northeastern wall recede into the afternoon sunlight. Each archway delineates a distinct firing position. Had an enemy ship ever approached—and had the fort ever been armed to its full potential—this design would have allowed 125 guns to zero on any given target all at once.

In the distance, the Garden Key harbor light (1876) sits atop the southeast bastion. It replaced an earlier freestanding lighthouse with a troubled history of inadequacies. Though multiple ships sank on its watch, Congress declined to replace or improve it. It was finally done in by a quick succession of violent hurricanes, making way for the current, improved light.

As seen from above, the parade ground is wild and mangy. Fort Jefferson is a behemoth, a prize-fighter who never met his match, never had his day in the ring—a contender now past his prime and gone to seed. The fort has never been attacked.

Each bastion tower contains gunrooms, magazines, and a granite spiral staircase leading from the parade all the way up to the barbette tier. By design, the spiral steps are considerably narrower at the inside than the outside—a last-ditch defensive measure to throttle traffic up the staircase should intruders ever breach the fort.

Traverse magazines appear as sixteen mounds ringing the barbette tier. Heavily reinforced, they were designed to shield the guns on this level from incoming fire while also supplying them with ammunition. The enclosed section on the first tier is the curtain magazine, meant to house forty-three tons of power.

The onset of the Civil War disrupted supply chains for the incomplete and unarmed Fort Jefferson. The yellowish bricks that comprise the majority of the fort were produced near Pensacola, which was suddenly out-of-bounds in enemy hands. Construction was completed using red bricks sourced all the way from Maine, as seen near the top of the curtain wall.

Fort Jefferson is audacious in scale. It demands to be shot in widescreen. Vertically it can be described in geological terms.

Into those walls, the sediments of history—the coming of the Civil War, the abolition of slavery, the rise of wage labor—are demarcated as the epochal events that they were. Like a layer of ash from the catastrophic eruption of some ancient volcano, you can see where, four-fifths of the way up the wall, the jaundiced brick produced by enslaved hands in Pensacola gives way to a ruddy variety imported from Maine, baked by anonymous European immigrants and laid by Confederate prisoners of war.

The fort was largely stripped of its heavy guns and abandoned to the elements by the 1870s. A small caretaker force maintained the hospital as a quarantine station. During this period, it also served as a convenient coaling station for the navy's Caribbean operations. In fact, in 1898, Fort Jefferson supplied the USS *Maine* with the coal that would blow it sky high over Havana harbor just days later, igniting the Spanish-American War.

In 1908, the Dry Tortugas became a national wildlife refuge, and in 1992, a national park.

Until recently, you could walk around the entire fort on top of the counterscarp, or moat wall. Successive hurricanes have since shattered that wall, making a complete circuit possible only with snorkeling gear. Even as the National Park Service undertakes conservation projects on features of Fort Jefferson like the Garden Key Lighthouse, it's not hard to imagine a day in the near future when it's unsafe to climb up to the barbette tier.

Fort Jefferson is a relic, a brick-and-mortar *cul-de-sac* of war-making technology from a time before large caliber rifled artillery could penetrate such brittle walls, before a changing climate threatened to swamp the whole unrealistic scene.

Get on a seaplane, take a ferry—get to Fort Jefferson before antebellum becomes antediluvian.

An unimpressive foundation is all that is left of the massive thousand-man barracks that once stood next to the large parade magazine on the east side of the fort.

The parapet—a low defensive wall along the edge of the roof—would have offered a limited degree of protection to gunners on the barbette tier.

Since few guns were ever deployed to the fort, many second-tier casemates became prison cells. The fort's most famous inmate was Dr. Samuel Mudd, who aided a wounded John Wilkes Booth in his escape after Lincoln's assassination. After an attempted escape in the coal bunker of a supply ship, Mudd settled into life at the fort, helping to stem a yellow fever outbreak in 1867.

◄ This 10-inch rifled Parrott gun weighs 27,000 pounds and could fire a 300-pound projectile. While it was capable of hitting targets with a high degree of accuracy, it was also known to explode, posing an extreme hazard to those operating it. As a result, only around forty of this type were ever produced.

Following the Civil War, Fort Jefferson was repurposed as the U.S. Navy's most extravagant fueling station. The ruins of the north coaling dock (1898) remain as a popular snorkel spot. Beyond lies Bush Key, once a natural pen for hogs who supplied fresh meat to the soldiers stationed here, and now an important nesting area for seabirds.

Each of the freestanding officers' quarters along the northwest end of the parade featured detached kitchens and outhouses. Despite the prevalence of diseases like yellow fever and scurvy, as well as the persistent threat from heat and hurricanes, some officers brought their families to live at remote Fort Jefferson.

Like all the gunports at Fort Jefferson, this iron-reinforced embrasure once featured Totten shutters. These iron shutters would be forced open by the rush of gas produced by a firing artillery piece then rebound shut immediately, shielding the gunners from any incoming fire.

The interior of each bastion offered gunners equipped with twelve 24-pounder flank defense howitzers the chance to fire parallel to the fort's curtain walls—a blistering measure against any attack that might penetrate into the 70-foot wide moat.

These archways provide a passage between adjacent casemates inside the curtain walls and would have allowed for communication and the transfer of ammunition, even during a pitched battle.

The sally port is the only way in or out of Fort Jefferson. It was originally equipped with a massive drawbridge. If an intruder managed to clear this obstacle, they faced a deep, narrow passageway lined with loopholes and capped with a second heavy door.

During the Civil War, the fort was a convenient base of operations for the Union's Anaconda Plan—a staging ground for the Union Navy, who were tasked with inhibiting any foreign commerce from reaching Confederate-held ports on the mainland. It was also home to some 600 Union deserters and other prisoners.

Bastions such as the six at Fort Jefferson afford a wider range of fire for a fort's defenders. The iron Totten shutters that once shielded the fort's embrasures have been inelegantly removed, long ago scavenged and sold for scrap.

The counterscarp doubles as a breakwater, defending the fort not only from attack, but also from wave action and storm surge. Recent hurricanes have caused portions of the wall to collapse, making a complete circumnavigation of the fort possible only with the aid of a snorkel.

◀ The ineffectual Confederate Navy posed little threat to Fort Jefferson. A single credible demand was issued for its surrender in January 1861 by the captain of an armed Confederate schooner. The fort's Union commander successfully bluffed that he would destroy the ship unless it retreated; in reality, the unfinished fort possessed no artillery.

The last seaplane of the day sets down on the vast open waters surrounding the islets of the Dry Tortugas. These remote islands were so christened in 1513 by Ponce de León to denote the local abundance of sea turtles—his crew killed 170—and the lack of fresh water anywhere in the chain.

As the sun sets, daytrippers depart, but the fort isn't quite deserted. U.S. park rangers live in the fort full-time, receiving regular supply deliveries and the occasional hot pizza from Key West. Garden Key is also home to a primitive first-come, first-served campground.

# 3

# WEST MARTELLO TOWER,
## KEY WEST

A modern gazebo stands amidst the meticulously manicured ruins of the West Martello Tower, home of the Key West Garden Club since 1955. It is the clearest manifestation of the fort transformation from implement of war into a monument to harmony.

The Martello towers of Key West were conceived—like so many of Florida's coastal defenses—during a crisis of American confidence following the War of 1812. Nine towers were envisioned to turn the entire island into a veritable fortress—the anvil to Fort Jefferson's hammer in defense of U.S. shipping lanes in the Gulf.

Urgent memories of the war faded, and these overly-ambitious, long-delayed plans were eventually scaled back, limited to Fort Zachary Taylor and the two towers, East and West, that stand today. Construction of the Martello towers finally commenced with the outbreak of Civil War. Despite the name, they are not true Martellos, which are round towers almost punk rock in their simplicity, allowing a single piece of artillery a 360-degree range of fire. Key West's are square and designed to house multiple artillery pieces—an American variant on the form or a simple misapplication of the term.

Before the war's end, the Union navy was firing newly-developed rifled artillery shells at brick forts across the Confederacy, shattering them like so many dainty champagne flutes. In the process, they rendered obsolete their own coastal defense system, including the unfinished Martellos.

The West Martello Tower was never completed—its brittle red brick walls a casualty of the sea change in defensive technology brought on by the advent of rifled artillery. Battered by the leading edge of a powerful hurricane, the outpost was gradually cannibalized, its component bricks repurposed into local construction projects.

Martellos are technically defined as free-standing cylindrical towers allowing a 360-degree range of fire. This fort, comprised of a rectangular central citadel protected by brick curtain walls typical of its Third System (1821-1867) vintage, is not a true Martello.

Occupying prime real estate on Atlantic Boulevard, where White Street meets the Straits of Florida, the West Martello Tower has been a garden far longer than it ever served any military purpose.

The West Martello Tower is situated on Higgs Beach on the south side of Key West, two miles down the coast from its sister, the East Martello Tower. Together, the two towers were intended to defend Key West's southern coast against an enemy landing. In fact, the earliest plans called for a ring of similar forts around the whole island.

The international slave trade persisted long after it became illegal. In 1860, three ships smuggling 1,500 Africans were intercepted by the U.S. Navy and diverted to the nearest port—Key West. Here, hundreds died as a consequence of the appalling conditions of their captivity. The fort stands vigil over the African Refugee Cemetery, their final resting place.

The West Martello Tower is one of the few free tourist attractions in all of Key West, offering a shady reprieve from the heat and clamor of Duval Street. Donations are gratefully accepted.

Battery Inman (1906) was an Endicott Period concrete coastal battery built within the remnants of the West Martello. It was equipped with two 3-inch M1903 guns on pedestal mounts, both scrapped in 1945. Under the auspices of the garden club, this emplacement has morphed into a terraced patio complete with pergola.

The central tower was slated to stand thirty-six feet tall. Though diminished, it still provides a winsome centerpiece for weddings and other celebrations.

So, the West Martello Tower was never completed. Instead, it fell into disuse, occupying valuable beach real estate, consigned to a sorry fate as the *de facto* black-market quarry for the denizens of the once and future-Conch Republic.

But who decided to turn this fort into a flowerpot?

In 1955, in a turn befitting a Hemingway tale of aged warriors and faded glory, a historically-minded County Commissioner named Joe Allen turned West Martello Tower over to the then-itinerant Key West Garden Club, who gladly fixed it up and still call it home today.

Such grand poetic gestures are rarely the stock-in-trade of locally-elected officials or garden clubs—but there you have it.

A peace garden stands between two large batteries. One of those batteries has been converted into a patio. The other houses rain barrels and an irrigation system which give life to the whole garden.

Out with the weapons of war, and in with orchids and bromeliads. Swords into plowshares, and everything nice.

Indigenous flora adorn the fractured remnants of the West Martello Tower. After 1955, the tireless members of the Key West Garden Club tidied up as best they could, removing debris from the fort by hand.

West Martello Tower was built as a redoubt for the much larger Fort Zachary Taylor, guarding against any aggressors who might approach from the east. Today, Fort Zachary Taylor is the bigger tourist draw—but the Martello offers the more unconventional experience.

Key West remained in Union hands throughout the Civil War. It was the home base for some forty warships which together intercepted more than two hundred Confederate-affiliated blockade runners during the course of the four-year conflict.

The Key West Garden Club has made only modest modifications to the ruined fort, which was placed on the U.S. National Register of Historic Places in 1976. The East Martello Tower gained the same honor in 1972. It is the better preserved of the two—home to a history and art museum centered on Key West generally.

The community peace garden—complete with a structure evocative of a Shinto torii and an inscription reading "We are all the keys to peace"—now inhabits the space between Battery Inman's two-gun emplacements.

The Key West Garden Club's mission is educational as well as aesthetic. Past projects include work with the Florida Department of Forestry promoting the propagation of native trees.

The vaulted casemates of West Martello Tower still cut a striking profile. Originally, they served a defensive purpose while housing powder and other military supplies. They now function as garden sheds, meeting space, and nurseries.

The Key West Garden Club maintains an extensive collection of documents pertaining to the history of the West Martello—and a comfortable environment in which to pore over them.

# 4

# FORT BARRANCAS,
## PENSACOLA

Fort Barrancas is a Third System fort located on the bluffs above Pensacola Bay, occupying the site of an earlier Spanish fortification made of wood. Built under harsh conditions by enslaved laborers between 1839 and 1844, the revamped brick Barrancas supplemented Forts McRee and Pickens in defense of the Pensacola Navy Yard, the U.S.'s primary shipbuilding facility on the Gulf.

F ort Barrancas was one of a trio of Third System forts built to defend the navy yard on Pensacola Bay, an installation vital for the maintenance of a U.S. naval presence in the Gulf of Mexico. It saw action, like so many of Florida's coastal defenses, not against some transatlantic foe, but in the bitter contest between two versions of America itself.

On January 8, 1861, three months before the Civil War erupted in earnest, a contingent of Florida militia aligned with the burgeoning Confederacy demanded the surrender of Fort Barrancas, then defended by a peacetime garrison of some fifty Union soldiers. These Union troops responded with a volley of fire, forcing the militia to retreat. In short order, the Yankees spiked Barrancas's large guns, loaded everything they could carry onto flatboat, and complied with the Confederate request.

It was in their strategic interest: Fort Pickens stood across the bay on the barrier island of Santa Rosa, offering this wayward unit a wider range of defensive fire and a better chance of reinforcement should the Union choose to come to their aid.

It is worth noting that this marks one of the few instances when a Confederate force in Florida took possession of a coastal fort; this possession, as elsewhere, was tenuous, circumstantial, and fleeting.

"Barranca" is Spanish for "bluffs," the natural feature which enhanced the ability of these cannons and mortars to rain iron fury upon any intruder threatening Pensacola Bay. In the distance rises the man-made glacis which guarded the rear, land-side approach to the fort, absorbing the impact of any hostile artillery fire and compelling the enemy force to fight uphill.

The central portion of Fort Barrancas has four sides, the two longest of which are protected by a deep dry ditch. The far side of the ditch is the counterscarp, which sits under the glacis and is connected to the main fort via a buried tunnel that runs parallel to the drawbridge.

The scarp gallery runs along the interior of the main fort's four walls. Loopholes were designed for muskets, allowing the defending garrison to fire with impunity upon any unfortunate assailants in the ditch outside. The arched casemates support the parapet above, which shielded emplacements on the parade for a combined twenty-six cannons, mortars, and howitzers.

This embrasure in the counterscarp allowed gunners to fire chain shot or cannister from a flank howitzer down the narrow confines of the ditch—devastating any attackers within.

On November 22, 1861, and again on January 1, 1862, Barrancas and its sister, Fort McRee, both in Confederate hands, exchanged heavy fire with Pickens and several ships that had arrived to support the Union position there. When the dust settled, Fort McRee had been devastated by state-of-the-art rifled artillery from the Union ships. Today its ruins sit beneath the waves. Forts Barrancas and Pickens, armed with traditional cannons and positioned at a distance to augment—not destroy—each other, were largely undamaged. Eyewitnesses describe shots rolling in with all of the velocity and menace of bowling balls.

The tide of the larger war, if ever it was in favor of the Confederacy, was turning. They soon abandoned Barrancas with no further struggle.

It's a good thing that these civil warriors took almost as much care with the historic real estate as do the modern park rangers. Today, Fort Barrancas, which incorporates an earlier Spanish battery designed to skip cannonballs like stones across the surface of the water at enemy ships, as well as a lethal scarp-counter-scarp configuration devised to thwart any ground-based attack, is one of the best preserved Third System forts anywhere in the country.

The v-shaped counterscarp gallery covered the longest sides of the fort. It was whitewashed to maximize ambient illumination. The triangular vents above the musket loopholes allowed for better ventilation. Dozens of guns firing in rapid succession could otherwise create a lethal, lingering cloud of smoke, asphyxiating the fort's defenders.

Powder was stored in one of half a dozen magazines located strategically throughout the fort. These magazines—like others of the day—were lined with wood instead of brick, and all attendants were required to forgo belt buckles and shoes—life-or-death precautions to avoid any chance of an accidental spark, which might blow Barrancas sky high from within.

A deep tunnel from the parade leads downhill to the water battery Bateria de San Antonio (1797)—the only part of the Spanish fort retained by the Americans. Most of the time, these fortifications were manned by a skeleton crew—the full garrison lived outside the walls in nearby barracks.

The water battery was set low on the bluffs, allowing the defending garrison to skip cannonballs across the surface of Pensacola Bay—like so many stones—with the goal of striking an enemy ship at the water line. With skill and luck, such a well-placed blow could cripple a hostile target at a range of up to one mile.

The water battery had a dedicated powder magazine insulated behind several thick walls and heavy doors. Above the magazine, atop a steep set of stairs, was a fire control platform which once offered a commanding view of the bay—obscured in modern times by a healthy stand of trees.

The water battery was equipped with eleven 32-pounder cannons, two 8-inch seacoast howitzers, and two 10-inch mortars. A cannon would pivot on the block near the wall, while the back end of the mount ran on wheels over these semi-circular traverse stones.

The Advanced Redoubt, built between 1845 and 1870, lies north of Barrancas proper. Operating together, the two outposts were meant to halt any land-based assault on the Pensacola Navy Yard to the east. The redoubt incorporates a complex system of scarp, counterscarp, glacis, demibastion, and traverses—the end result of centuries of defensive engineering against attack by cannonballs and muskets.

Engineers struggled against technological limits to improve on the Third System in the latter half of the 1800s, ▶ eventually devising the next generation Endicott Period batteries built of reinforced concrete. Today, the redoubt, along with the rest of Fort Barrancas, resides within Naval Air Station Pensacola, itself a state-of-the-art representation of U.S. coastal defense in the twenty-first century.

The First System of coastal defense was mostly low-walled fortifications of earth and wood, hastily executed during the Revolutionary War. The Second System—casemated brick forts—was developed without urgency between 1789 and 1812. The Third System capitalized on lessons learned in earlier conflicts—but all forty-two forts built under this program were obsolete by the end of the Civil War.

# 5

# FORT PICKENS,
## PENSACOLA

Fort Pickens, built largely by enslaved laborers between 1829 and 1834, was a five-sided Third System fort with mounts for two hundred cannon and room for a thousand men. It was comprised of fifty-eight casemates on the first level (exposed here), five bastions, a barbette tier, and a three-sided counterscarp guarding its rear approach.

What furious trumpet blast—what indomitable enemy—could have shattered these once mighty walls?

Broken and humble as it is today, Fort Pickens is a marvel of engineering—a Third System fort, augmented by seven Endicott Period batteries and three more built during World War II, it guarded Pensacola Bay for over a century. A fortification inspired by the War of 1812 and built by slaves between 1829 and

1834, Fort Pickens repelled successive Confederate attacks to remain in Union hands throughout the entirety of the Civil War. It later held the infamous Geronimo as a captive and honest-to-God beachside tourist attraction between 1886 and 1887. Two generations later, it guarded Pensacola and its navy yard from the likes of Nazi U-boats—before its final retirement in 1947.

That's a solid record of service for a castle built on sand. To support the tremendous weight of the 21.5 million bricks that make up Fort Pickens, all passageways in the fort are arched not just at the top, but on the bottom as well. These reverse arches extend underground, providing more than enough stability to keep the fort's walls and its expansive artillery casemates open to the public even two centuries after its initial construction—an ingenious solution laid on the foundation of ancient architectural principles.

Fort Pickens is like your grandfather, a man you knew only in the twilight of his old age, weary and worn—a man who, in truth, lived a life of action longer and fuller than you can imagine.

Fort Pickens, as seen from atop Bastion C, sits on the far west end of Santa Rosa Island near Pensacola Pass. Fort McRee formerly anchored the east end of Perdido Key across the channel, and Fort Barrancas clung to the bluffs above. Together, they created a web of interlocking fire controlling the approach to Pensacola Navy Yard, where the Gulf fleet was serviced.

Bastion D no longer exists, except in the historical record. On the night of June 20, 1899, a fire burned out of control, reaching one of the fort's three powder magazines located inside the bastion. Eight thousand pounds of powder ignited and the resulting explosion shattered the north end of the fort, raining bricks and other debris over Pensacola Bay.

So, what awesome calamity could have befallen this stolid American Jericho?

Early in the morning on June 20, 1899, a fire burned out of control. The blaze grew in heat and intensity, resisting all efforts by the men present to extinguish it. By 5:20 a.m., the flames had reached the magazine in bastion D—some 8,000 pounds of powder exploded with enough force to drop debris on Fort Barrancas a mile and half across the bay.

Earthbound stone, heaven sent.

Soon after, the fire was brought under control.

Since brick-and-mortar walls offered almost no defense against the more accurate and powerful rifled shells of the day, the army leaned in on the damage. To better supply the Endicott-era battery occupying the fort's parade ground, they paved a road where the wall once stood.

When you play with fire, you will sometimes get burned.

Fort Pickens is 21.5 million bricks, minus a few.

After the explosion, the army built a roadway through the gap in Fort Pickens's north wall. Hulking Fort Pickens was reduced to a mere support role for Battery Pensacola (1898), a far more powerful Endicott battery with two 12" M1895 guns mounted on disappearing M1897 carriages built on Pickens's parade.

The gaping hole where Bastion D once stood is now the fort's most distinguishing feature. In 1861, after state militia captured the navy yard on behalf of a seceding Florida, defiant U.S. soldiers displayed a large American flag from Bastion D—clearly visible to the rebels a short distance across the bay. Pickens was the only fort in Pensacola to remain in Union hands throughout the war.

Disasters notwithstanding, Fort Pickens has proven to be a remarkably durable structure under harsh, oceanfront conditions. In part, this stability can be attributed to the use of an ingenious reverse arch structure, which distributes evenly the immense weight of the fort above, minimizing settling in the sandy substrate which undergirds the entire structure.

Embrasures inside Bastion B seem to glow ominously in the late afternoon sun. These embrasures allowed gunners to fire flank howitzers down the length of the curtain wall, defending against a land-based attack.

Two large cannons remain on the barbette tier—most strikingly, a 15-inch Rodman cannon capable of firing a 440-pound projectile up to three miles. Crews of seven men used tools including a rammer, sponge, quadrant, shell hook, and carrying bar to clean, load, position, and fire this 50,000-pound beast. The heavy carriage rotated on wheels and absorbed the gun's massive recoil.

The parapet shields one of dozens of firing positions on the barbette tier. The iron nub on the pedestal is an anchor point—called a pintle—around which the Rodman occupying this position would have pivoted.

In 1884, this 10-inch Rodman smoothbore from 1861 was retrofitted with an 8-inch rifled sleeve—a stopgap measure to modernize the guns at Fort Pickens and extend their service life. Though of a smaller caliber, these new 8-inch rifled shells could fly farther with greater accuracy and force than the balls once fired from this weapon.

Eventually the army had to concede the reality that Fort Pickens was hopelessly out of date no matter how many modifications were made to its decades-old armaments. Battery Pensacola, like all next generation Endicott Period batteries, was built from reinforced concrete, shielded behind an earthen mound, and equipped with large-caliber rifled artillery.

The walls of Pickens standing south of Battery Pensacola, as useful against rifled artillery as a shield of fine china, were inelegantly trimmed down to provide the Endicott battery with an unobstructed line of fire on targets up to eight miles distant in the Gulf of Mexico.

The 12-inch rifled shells fired from Battery Pensacola weighed 1,070 pounds each. Overhead rails and a shell hoist system moved the heavy projectiles around and from the lower level—where magazines, generators, and other support rooms were located—to the loading level—where the two emplacements and fire control tower were located.

At Battery Pensacola, late afternoon sunlight floods down a stairwell into the lower-level magazine.

During the Endicott Period, the casemates of Fort Pickens were retrofitted to support a mining operation that could seal Pensacola Pass on short notice. Such systems became integral to coastal defense during the era of ironclads and armored cruisers.

The area surrounding Fort Pickens is now home to the beautiful Gulf Islands National Seashore. This entire end of Santa Rosa Island is punctuated by an ellipsis of seven Endicott Period batteries—largely resembling Battery Pensacola—which were employed from the turn of the twentieth century through World War II.

Battery Langdon (1917)—camouflaged beneath a mound of sand and vegetation—was the largest battery built during Pickens's twilight. Its 12-inch guns could fire a shell seventeen miles out to sea. According to the National Park Service, crews stationed at the battery though World War II reported split pants and bleeding from the mouth and ears when the gun fired.

# 6

# FORT DADE,
## EGMONT KEY

In 1849, Robert E. Lee recommended that Egmont Key be reserved for possible defensive works to guard Tampa Bay should future trade and settlement in the area ever warrant such an expense. The region is now one of Florida's most densely populated, and Egmont Key is a favorite weekend destination for boaters.

S lender, sandy, and shrinking, Egmont Key guards the entrance to Tampa Bay on Florida's Suncoast. It's home to a lighthouse and a long history as a U.S. military outpost. During the Third Seminole War (1855–1858), it served as a temporary internment camp for Seminoles, a convenient and isolated waystation before their forced removal from the state. Referred to in army documents as an "Indian depot," it was to modern eyes a concentration camp—a wooden stockade holding neither prisoners of war nor criminals, but men, women, and children of an undesirable race. At least five members of the tribe died while interred here—this would-be purgatory, a final destination. Along with a few dozen members of the U.S. armed services from across the decades, they are memorialized under simple wooden crosses in the scrubby Egmont Key Lighthouse Cemetery.

In the twenty-first century, this cemetery, like the history of the island, is all but forgotten, swamped by the rising tide of snowbirds and transplants who have adopted Florida as their new, air-conditioned home. To them, Florida is a paradise without baggage.

One sunny Saturday morning in May, I catch the regular ferry from Fort DeSoto County Park to work on behalf of the Egmont Key Alliance, an all-volunteer organization dedicated to restoring, preserving, and protecting Egmont Key and all of its resources, both natural and man-made. I'm not an active member of the Alliance, but I applaud their Sisyphean efforts. Once a month, they spread out over the historical ruins on the north end of this island, performing vital conservation and maintenance work.

At the time of its construction, the power plant (1919) was near the center of the island. Swift channel currents to the north and south are sweeping Egmont Key off the map. To the south, two of the fort's batteries—Burchsted and Page—have already slipped beneath the lukewarm and indifferent waves of the Gulf.

The one-mile Palmetto Trail (1905) runs along the eastern, protected side of the island which faces Tampa Bay. Its red brick surface once conveyed personnel and materiel from the quartermaster's wharf to the cantonment near the island's midpoint.

An organizer assigns to me the task of tending that little graveyard, and I spend a better part of the day amongst those woebegone graves, pinching and pulling the weeds that threaten to overtake the blemished sand of this humble plot. The past is rarely forgotten in grand, sweeping acts of erasure. Rather, it's the little things—peeling paint, the sliding of sand into the sea, the hearty plants that gain a foothold in cracked concrete—it's these seemingly benign markers of time that subsume our collective memory.

During the Civil War, the Union retained control of Egmont Key, using the 87-foot lighthouse as a watchtower to spot Confederate blockade runners coming and going from Tampa Bay. In this capacity, Egmont Key was instrumental in the Union's larger war aim—its Anaconda Plan—of maintaining a chokehold on a Confederate economy highly dependent on the importation of foreign manufactured goods. But even at this late date, and despite the onset of open war, there were no formal military fortifications on the island.

Egmont Key Lighthouse Cemetery was once the resting place of U.S. servicemen who died on the island. Markers also commemorate Seminole tribe members who died in detention while awaiting a forced removal to Indian Territory. All bodies known to be interred on Egmont Key were relocated to St. Augustine National Cemetery in 1909.

Egmont Key Lighthouse stands 87 feet tall and dates to 1858, the only structure on the island to survive from the period of the Seminole Wars. During the Civil War, its lens was stolen by Confederates in an effort to frustrate the Union Navy, who otherwise maintained control of Egmont Key.

All of that changed with the Spanish American War. Visions of American empire abroad inspired a sense of vulnerability at home, spurring the construction of more formidable defenses along the U.S. coastline. By 1898, the city of Tampa, with its deepwater port and well-developed rail lines, was a vital embarkation point for troops and supplies headed to Cuba. To defend the city, the army established Fort Dade on Egmont Key and its sister, Fort DeSoto on Mullet Key. Fort Dade was comprised of five concrete batteries, each deploying multiple large guns capable of lobbing heavy shells at targets up to five miles distant. The two forts sit about a mile apart, positioned to create a bowel-shaking web of interlocking fire convergent on the main shipping channel.

What's left of Fort Dade today lies in ruins along the northwest shore of Egmont Key, crumbling in the debilitating heat and humidity of the Gulf Coast. The batteries have long since fallen into an ethereal silence, their guns deployed elsewhere during World War I or on display in an open-air museum at Fort DeSoto.

Visitors can scramble freely atop what remains of these disarmed sentries, standing watch over breathtaking views of the Gulf. Down below, where little of the sun's light reaches, they can explore various underground compartments once used for the storage of powder and shells. Rainwater regularly collects in stagnant puddles, which evaporate slowly in the thick air.

Fort Dade features all the hallmarks of Endicott Period (1895-1910) coastal defense, which abandoned a conventional enclosed fortress design in favor of dispersed emplacements. These were equipped with rifled artillery mounted on disappearing carriages which hid them from enemy fire.

Battery James McIntosh (1898) was constructed from reinforced concrete and equipped with two 8-inch M1888MI guns seated on an elevated platform facing the Gulf of Mexico.

The powder magazine, guardhouse, and plotting room of Battery McIntosh were located on the ground level. Ammunition was supplied to second-level firing positions through two hoist wells. In 1923, both artillery pieces were removed, and the battery was decommissioned.

Endicott Period emplacements were typically camouflaged from enemy observation and shielded from fire behind large earthen embankments. From the Gulf, Battery McIntosh looks like any grass-covered dune; from the island, its concrete form evokes some waggish Art Nouveau playground, gnarled beyond recognition.

Egmont Key is now a National Wildlife Refuge. Its tranquility is broken only by the careless chatter of occasional daytrippers. Frat boys, home for summer break, wander up from the beach, teasing their bikinied girlfriends with a virility incubated in the intense Florida sun. They suggest that the girls are too scared to go into these labyrinths, dark and dank, but amidst the laughter and playful jostling, those boisterous guys always seem to forget their own dare. They head back to the beach and their Bluetooth speakers.

This is the best chance they will ever get to travel through time, and it's utterly lost on them.

In its prime, Fort Dade was home to two casemates stocked full of mines, ready— under threat of an enemy incursion—for deployment across the mouth of Tampa Bay at a moment's notice. Jungle growth swallows whole the support facilities for this mining operation, leaving behind nothing but the digested skeletons of structures which once housed enough explosive force to erase half of Egmont Key at a blow.

May we all outlive our purpose in life, if our purpose be so cruel.

Red roof tiles lie shattered on the concrete. Towering palm trees offer the only shade, stretching sunward between staid block walls, themselves fractured but still standing, if only just barely.

The Fort Dade cantonment was composed primarily of wooden and brick structures. All that's left of the gymnasium (1909) is a trace of crumbled foundation overgrown with weeds. In later years, the gymnasium became a firing range, which accounts for the large number of shell casings in the vicinity.

Little remains of the once extensive cantonment beyond foundations such as these—a century of hurricanes, vandalism, and fires. On April 25, 1925, federal agents ignited grass fires in an effort to smoke out bootleggers hiding in the recently abandoned town, destroying eight homes, a coal storage facility, and the power plant.

The quartermaster's storehouses (1900) made daily life possible for the more than 200 men stationed on isolated Egmont Key. Today, this storehouse is one of the few structures outside of the batteries to remain intact in any form. In 1975, a fire caused by lightning seared its way across the island, consuming what remained of the cantonment.

These thirty-foot concrete pillars once supported the fire control command tower (1905). Located on the west side of Egmont Key and equipped with two telescopes, the tower gave officers a sweeping field of view over the Gulf of Mexico, allowing them to identify and triangulate enemy positions. These calculations were relayed to the batteries via telephone.

As these things often go, none of the ambitious war-waging facilities at Fort Dade were completed in time to be of any use in the short-lived conflict of 1898—the first heavy artillery at Egmont Key did not come online until 1900, and the fort was not deemed complete until 1910. By the mid-twenties, after a direct hit from a hurricane, in an era of increased American isolation, the entire base was all but abandoned.

A complement of more than 200 U.S. servicemen were stationed at isolated Fort Dade during its twenty-year heyday. The army built a sizeable cantonment to provide for their needs, including barracks for the enlisted men, as well as a neighborhood of freestanding homes for the officers. There was also segregated housing for African-American laborers and an elaborate infrastructure to service the logistical needs of the quartermaster. There was a movie theatre, a gym, and even a bowling alley.

After a century of sun and storms, most of this once robust town is gone, replaced with chaotic plots of heavy subtropical growth, neatly framed by a grid of red brick streets that call to mind some idyllic, well-to-do suburb of the day. But no matter how well they have aged, all roads on Egmont Key lead to the sweet oblivion of wilderness. This may be the most profound insight offered by the ruins of a fortress conceived in preparation for a war that never came—no matter how well men and nations plan for mastery over all who would challenge their dominance, nature gets every last one of them in the end.

A century of scorching sun and harsh humidity has laid bare the rebar skeleton of the quartermaster's storehouse. The earlier Seminole internment camp (1858) was built from wood, meaning that, as with so much from that period of conquest in Florida, almost no physical evidence remains to tell the tale.

The best modern conjecture says that the Seminole internment camp was located north of the cantonment, near—or perhaps under—the 1970s-vintage helipad. There's also a reasonable chance that it has already slid into the Gulf of Mexico, along with a poorly documented Seminole graveyard.

One remarkable story of Seminole resistance begins on Egmont Key in 1858, when Emateloye, aka Polly Parker, embarked as a prisoner on a steamer destined for Oklahoma. During a refueling stop in St. Marks, Emateloye led a daring escape, making the 300-mile journey home to Lake Okeechobee on foot in less than a week. A matriarch of Florida's modern Seminole nation, she lived free and unconquered until 1921.

This proposed maxim is truer at Egmont Key more than ever. The whole island is sliding into the Gulf of Mexico at a startling rate. It's been here at the juncture between the Gulf and Tampa Bay since at least the time of Spanish exploration, some 500 years ago. In the 1850s, a survey by the U.S. Army (conducted by none of other than Robert E. Lee) found Egmont Key to have an area of 580 acres. In recent years, the dwindling island tops out below 250 acres. These sandy keys along the Florida coast come and go, to be sure, but Egmont Key seems to have hit some kind of tipping point during the last decade. Beachfront structures are collapsing not on any kind of geological time scale, but between my visits.

Already, two batteries are accessible only with the aid of a snorkel. Experts say that the whole island could be gone in a few years if the right hurricane struck. The state has placed several temporary retaining walls along the northwest shore of the island.

In reality, this is only a stopgap measure, no more a defense against inexorable oblivion brought by the shifting sands of time than was the once mighty fortress that calls this island home.

Sand is suction dredged from the shipping channel, spewing forth from this massive pipe in a process called beach nourishment—an effort to stave off the effects of erosion and climate change at Fort Dade on Egmont Key.

Battery Guy Howard (1906) was equipped with two 6-inch M1903 rifles mounted on disappearing carriages. Magazines were located on the same level as the firing positions, so shells would have moved between on handcarts. During World War I, these guns were redeployed in support of American forces in France.

Resting on a foundation of shifting sand, with walls intersecting at precarious angles where they meet at all, the firing positions and magazines of Battery Howard are barely distinguishable from the landscape.

The various batteries of Fort Dade were linked by a narrow concrete road that still allows for an easy circuit of the historical part of the island.

The south end of Egmont Key became a National Wildlife Refuge in 1974 and is now home to 35,000 nesting birds, 1,200 gopher tortoises, and dozens of varieties of trees, grasses, and flowering plants.

Battery Charles Mellon (1904) stood on the north end of Egmont Key, guarding the shipping channel with three 3-inch M1898MI Driggs-Seabury guns on masking parapet mounts, a simpler form of disappearing carriage. These 3-inch guns were positioned to defend underwater mines in the channel against enemy minesweepers.

The exterior power plant housed a generator which supplied electricity to operations at Battery Mellon. During World War II, the island's batteries were called into use one last time in defense of Tampa Bay—outfitted with searchlights instead of guns to spot potential enemy activity off the coast.

Battery Mellon lies low, just feet from the water, and has been swamped during recent storms.

Battery Mellon forms an L-shape with magazines located on the lower level and guns on the second. All ammunition was moved between levels by hand, as no hoists were included in the battery's design.

The neutered gun emplacements at Battery Mellon offer a stunning view—the best place to watch the steady stream of more than 3,000 cargo and tanker ships calling at Port Tampa Bay annually.

The Fort Dade mine wharf (1916) allowed for the rapid deployment of mines across the deepwater shipping channel, effectively sealing the bay in the event of an enemy's approach. Mines were dispatched from storage to the wharf along a small steam powered railway.

◄ Since the main fire control tower could not provide adequate visual coverage over the shipping channel—where Battery Mellon's field of fire was concentrated—a second, dedicated control tower was built on the north end of the island.

These hulking structures—the cable tank and mine storehouses (1908)—once supplemented the mining operation at the north end of Egmont Key. In the event of actual deployment, the mines would be armed, controlled, and detonated from a concrete-reinforced casemate buried nearby under a mound of dirt.

The cable tank and mine storehouses were each equipped with a large overhead crane. Today, all that stands overhead is an ever-thickening canopy of trees. A similar compound once existed at the south end of the island, but has since slipped into the sea.

The two buildings held the electrical cables, mine cases, anchors, and buoys necessary to deploy and arm the minefield. As fate would have it, none of this equipment ever proved necessary in Tampa Bay and was only ever handled during drills.

The electrical cables that controlled the mines would corrode easily in open air during long periods of disuse. To prevent such degradation, they were stored on reels in large tanks of fresh water.

# 7

# NIKE MISSILE SITE HM-69,
## EVERGLADES NATIONAL PARK

A relic of heightened thermonuclear tensions, this Nike-Hercules missile sits on display in one of the three barns at HM-69 in Everglades National Park. Armed and fueled, the 41-foot-long missile weighed 11,000 pounds and represented the U.S.'s last line of defense against nuclear attack from the south.

D eep in the remote heart of the Everglades, in the midst of a rolling sawgrass marsh, mere feet above sea level, on a plot of land with the forlorn epithet Hole-in-the-Donut, behind a nondescript berm and a chain link fence, sits Alpha Battery, Nike Missile Base HM-69—from 1964 to 1979, a vital component of the U.S.'s nuclear defense.

This is what coastal defense looked like during the atomic age. By the 1960s, no one expected an invasion from the sea anymore. State-of-the-art radar arrays had replaced masonry lookout towers. Our eyes were trained on the sky, and this was our best guess at what an advanced redoubt for the end of the world was going to look like.

Hole-in-the-Donut is a cheeky name offered up by the ecologists who manage Everglades National Park, a nod to the fact that this parcel was once 6,000 acres of farmland, tilled, disturbed, and now overrun with the invasive and tenacious Brazilian pepper—a man-made mess in the middle of the otherwise pristine river of grass.

About 140 men of the 2nd Battalion, 52nd Air Defense Artillery were stationed here at any given time, tasked with one of the grimmest missions ever devised by man. In the event of a Soviet nuclear strike from Cuba or some other southerly point of origin, the servicemen consigned to this swamp would be charged with hurtling aloft a barrage of Nike Hercules missiles designed to intercept and incapacitate the enemy offensive *enroute*. Some of these interceptors—41 feet long and ready to launch at a moment's notice—were themselves tipped with 20-kt nuclear warheads.

The Homestead–Miami Defense Area (HM), established in the wake of the Cuban Missile Crisis, was composed of a dozen Nike missile batteries spread over the southeast corner of Florida. HM-69, on Long Pine Key Road in Everglades National Park, is the farthest west of these bases—and in the modern day, the best preserved.

At any given moment during its heyday, HM-69 was home to 140 members of the 2nd Battalion, 52nd Air Defense Artillery, ready for action at a moment's notice. The base consisted of twenty-two structures including barracks, a guard dog kennel, a guardhouse, radar units, and this building used for missile assembly.

HM-69's Nike Hercules missiles would leave their hydraulic-articulated launch rails at roughly the speed of sound. Every moment would count. A supersonic flight from Cuba to Florida by MiG, bomber, or ballistic missile, after all, would take only minutes, placing the entire Eastern seaboard in peril. That impressive 20-kt yield—roughly the size of the bomb that destroyed Nagasaki—meant that even the relatively imprecise guidance technology of the 1960s had a reasonable chance of taking a Soviet target out of the sky.

Best case scenario, though, if we're being realistic—a successful launch from HM-69 wouldn't really save many lives. Rather, it would serve only to mitigate the opening volley of World War III, buying time to launch a full-scale U.S. counteroffensive. Given the massive firepower arrayed on both sides—in 1965, upwards of 30,000 weapons deployed by the U.S. and over 6,000 by the Soviet Union—and the stated, ongoing commitment in both Moscow and Washington to the suicide pact that is mutually assured destruction—well …

If this is the best plan we've got for the survival of the species …

Miami or Washington might survive an extra ten or twenty minutes before the second wave came crashing down. In that time, perhaps the President and a few members of Congress could make it to safety. Regardless, it would be the last day of life on Earth as we know it.

So, even after a job well done, even after mission accomplished, there wouldn't be much left for the men at HM-69 to do except to crack open a C-ration—maybe a can of Schlitz—and watch the distant world burn from the relative isolation of their swampy refuge, knowing that they'd done their best to stamp out an ember or two.

Thankfully, that nightmare never came to pass. Despite a constant state of readiness and an impeccable record of service under implacable conditions, HM-69 never fired a single shot in anger.

Archival photos show crews drilling in flood waters up over their ankles. This is Florida at its rawest, in the middle of nowhere with the gators and wading birds, seemingly a whole planet away from the postcard beach resorts. A Hole-in-the-Donut indeed.

Over time, the nickname became interchangeable with the base itself, an example of the wry, fatalistic humor that many U.S. servicemen acquire when asked time and again to carry out the most inscrutable duties in the name of service to country. A hole in a donut is something defined by what it isn't—an aptly nihilistic descriptor if I've ever heard one for a place designed for a function we hoped it would never perform.

HM-69—also sometimes referred to as Battery A—featured three above-ground launch units, each with four missiles. Under normal conditions, Nike Hercules missiles were stored in a safe mode. During an alert, crews would roll missiles out of the sliding doors and load them onto a hydraulic rail from which they would launch—at the speed of sound—into the sky.

The heavy blast doors of the missile barn were designed to withstand the full force of a missile's rockets during launch. Volunteers have banded together as the Friends of Everglades Nike Site to offer regular interpretive tours and perform basic restoration and maintenance on the remnants of the base.

Today, authority over HM-69 resides with Everglades National Park, which opens the decommissioned base during the dry season between early December and late March.

Three missile hangars, a missile assembly building, a guard dog kennel, barracks, and bunkers are all still here, the worse for wear after decades of little maintenance.

But it's not the heat, it's the humidity.

Heavy, blast-resistant doors are rusting off their hinges, so the boldest explorers can easily gain access to all three hangars, even though only the first one is officially open to visitors. It houses a decommissioned Nike Hercules missile, impressive even in its neutered state, as well as ephemera ranging from control and guidance equipment to a Cheerios box offering toy Nike missiles to the lucky kids of the 1960s. A wacky Cold War promotion designed to further the cause of patriotism and to normalize a feeling of low-level existential dread in the suburbs? "Hey kids, you don't have to wait for nuclear Ragnarök—now you can act it out at home!"

Each missile barn was paired with its own launch pad and tucked into a u-shaped berm meant to contain the explosive force of a launch. This berm was built over a concrete and asbestos-lined bunker. In the event of a launch, six-man support crews would seek shelter inside.

A secondary escape hatch provided the sheltering crew an alternative exit from the bunker should the primary door be obstructed by fire or debris kicked up during a Hercules launch.

Ventilation shafts allowed sheltering crews access to fresh air; radios would be their only line of communication with the outside world—if the outside world still existed at all. Fire control was supplied from a nearby building, which is now the National Park Service's Daniel Beard Research Center. From there, NPS coordinates efforts to repel a different kind of modern-day invasion—that of the Burmese python in the Everglades.

The launch bunkers are off limits even to the most adventurous. From a certain point of view, they look like rolling hills—totally out of place in the vast flatlands of south Florida. Walk around to the other side—facing away from the cracked concrete of the launch pad—and you notice long ventilation shafts erupting out of overgrown grass. They are unnatural, like an intubated patient in intensive care. There are heavy blast doors, too, sealed tight and carved right into the hillside, like forbidden portals to more haunting secrets inside. This is where crews would have sheltered, riding out the launch from the comfort of a sand-covered, concrete-reinforced, asbestos-lined bunker. It's where their nightmare would have ensued, had they ever been called upon to put their training into action.

I'm about to scramble up top through the high grass for a better view of the launch pad, but I notice a number of snake skins underfoot, freshly shed and seemingly everywhere. The thought of placing hand or foot down upon a possibly venomous snake—it's a bit too much adventure for one day…

Besides, the park ranger is coming. Long gone are the days when this place was on twenty-four-hour alert. The base is closing for the day, and he needs to lock the gate.

The Nike Hercules was hurled aloft by the XM-42, a bundle of four boosters adapted from the earlier Nike Ajax series of missile. The Hercules had a range of 75 miles and an operational altitude between 20,000 and 150,000 feet. Its top speed was Mach 3.65, or 2,707 mph.

An overhead track for the sliding barn doors is corroded but still functional. The doors are opened semi-regularly for tours and ranger access to a smattering of equipment stored inside.

LOCK DOOR
IMMEDIATLEY
UPON ENTRY

HM-69 was deactivated in 1979 and added to the Register of Historic Places in 2004. Meanwhile, the harsh humidity of the Everglades and years of neglect have taken their toll; the service door on this missile barn is rusting off of its hinges.

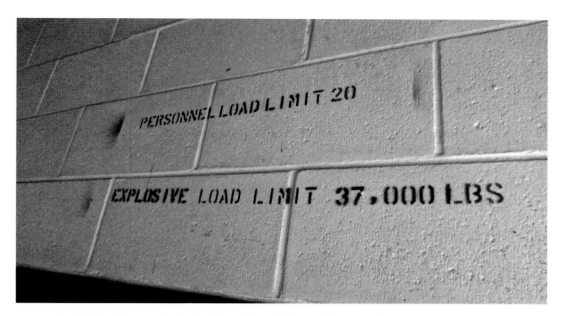

A notice like this one, stenciled on the inside wall of a missile barn, could save lives. Most of HM-69's sister sites have been demolished in favor of civilian construction or over safety concerns after damage in successive south Florida hurricanes.

The hydraulic launch systems once so central to the mission of HM-69 were long ago dismantled and removed from their concrete pads. The NPS boat trailer occupying that space is used to monitor invasive species such as the python or the tegu—exotic pets that, through negligence, have escaped and established breeding populations within the park.

In this book, you've read plenty of stats about the size and range of arms, about their hypothetical capacity to destroy, and about the hypothetical capacity of brick walls to resist.

All of it is true—carefully researched—but in a sense, it fails to capture *the truth*.

Because it's also true that the vast majority of those guns and walls—so mighty on paper and in field tests—were never measured in battle against any of the foes that inspired their construction. Why weren't these great weapons of war ever put to use against the British, the Spanish, or the Russians?

Was Florida never attacked by any of those supposed rivals because its defenses were so formidable? Was it because the threat these nations posed was largely imagined in the first place? Or because, to some degree in each case, goodwill ultimately superseded conflict?

Posed more directly, the question is, is military force—big, bold, and expensive—the most effective way to defend a country? It could be. At first glance, Florida seems to have a lot of fortifications along its coasts arguing in the affirmative. On the other hand, how many of these forts played a real and concrete role in other more dubious national accomplishments over the years—like the conquest of America from native peoples, the perpetuation of slavery, and the militarization of American culture? How often did they divert resources from humane endeavors like education, economic justice, or racial equality?

National defense comes at a cost.

And too often, our enemy doesn't come storming across the beach—he's already here, and he's done little more than ask a question about America that makes us uncomfortable.

* * *

It's a long drive back to Homestead, and I keep thinking about those unseen snakes, their cast-off skins a warning to anyone possessed of sufficient hubris to disrupt the peace.

> Beware, all who tread recklessly. We mean you no harm from our place in the sun, but we will respond in kind to any aggression.

It's a sentiment appropriate enough for the Seminole, the Spanish, a colony of free blacks, or anyone else through the centuries who's laid credible claim to a mushy patch of swampy Florida soil.

And it's a fitting epitaph for HM-69, a husk of its former, ferocious self—a monument to the madness of manmade conflict, perched alone in the animal wilderness of the Everglades. An odd and mostly forgotten collection of buildings, obsolete and arcane like so many others in the long line of fortifications that have guarded the Florida peninsula—a particularly solemn and lonely testament to the remarkable lengths to which a nation will go in the name of self-defense.

And I'm left wondering: When the wind blows, is the United States strong like the oak or like the grass?

The branch of the mighty oak snaps in the strongest wind, but after the rain the grass just grows greener. Fort Dade, Egmont Key.

# ABOUT THE AUTHOR

**THOMAS KENNING** is an author, educator, and adventurer. He holds an MA in history from American University in Washington, D.C., and teaches the subject in St. Petersburg, Florida. As a writer and photographer, he is passionate about documenting the vibrant history and stunning ecosystems of the Sunshine State. When he's not travelling to some far-flung corner of the Earth, Thomas resides with his wife and daughter—planning his next improbable adventure, sure, but also trying to leave the planet a little bit nicer than he found it.